COUNTRY HITS FOR THE TEEN PLAYER

EASY PIANO ARRANGEMENTS BY DAN COATES

CONTENTS

AMAZED
LONESTAR 2

THE DANCE
GARTH BROOKS 6

DON'T ROCK THE JUKEBOX
ALAN JACKSON 9

HOW DO I LIVE
LEANN RIMES 12

I SWEAR
JOHN MICHAEL MONTGOMERY 15

I'M TAKING THE WHEEL
SHEDAISY 19

INSIDE YOUR HEAVEN
CARRIE UNDERWOOD 23

JUST TO HEAR YOU SAY THAT YOU LOVE ME
FAITH HILL & TIM MCGRAW 27

LET ME LET GO
FAITH HILL 30

LIVE LIKE YOU WERE DYING
TIM MCGRAW 34

LOVE WILL ALWAYS WIN
GARTH BROOKS & TRISHA YEARWOOD . . 38

ONE MORE DAY
DIAMOND RIO 42

SOME HEARTS
CARRIE UNDERWOOD 45

SOMEBODY LIKE YOU
KEITH URBAN 48

SUNSHINE ON MY SHOULDERS
JOHN DENVER 51

THIS KISS
FAITH HILL 54

WHEN I THINK ABOUT ANGELS
JAMIE O'NEAL 59

DAN COATES® is a registered trademark of Alfred Publishing Co., Inc.

Copyright © MMVII by ALFRED PUBLISHING CO., INC.
All rights reserved.   Printed in USA.
ISBN-10: 0-7390-4290-4
ISBN-13: 978-0-7390-4290-8

AMAZED

Words and Music by Marv Green,
Aimee Mayo and Chris Lindsey
Arranged by Dan Coates

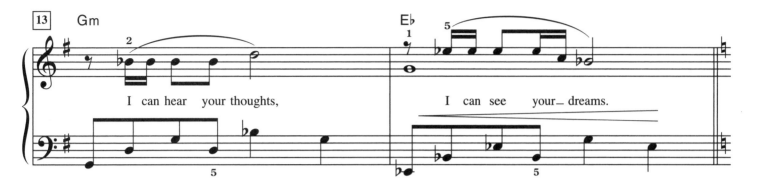

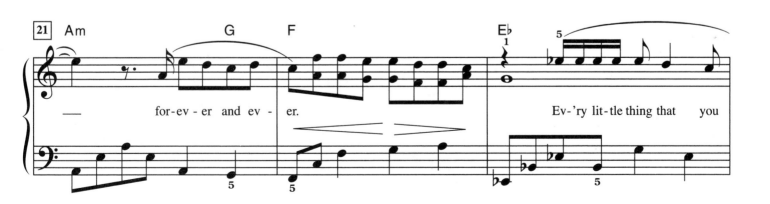

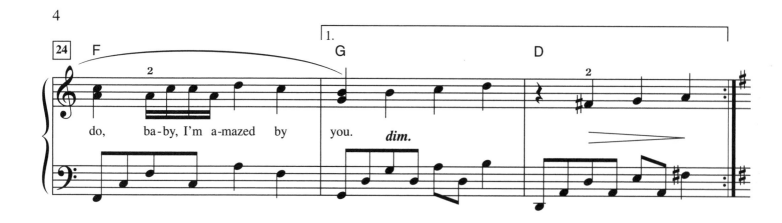

do, ba-by, I'm a-mazed by you. *dim.*

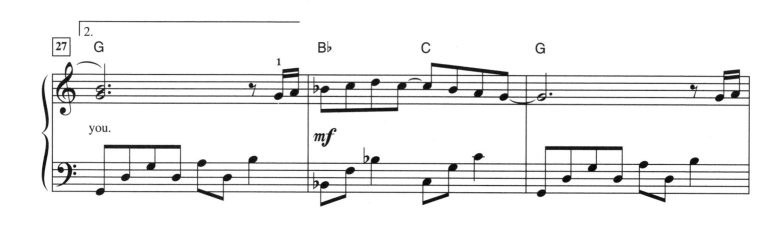

you. *mf*

f Ev-'ry lit-tle thing that you do,— I'm so in love with

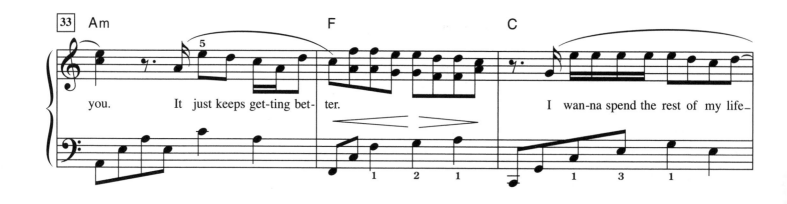

you. It just keeps get-ting bet-ter. I wan-na spend the rest of my life—

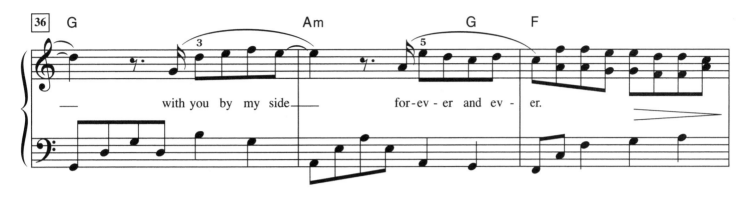

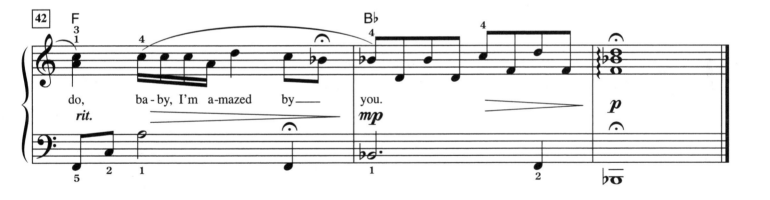

Verse 2:
The smell of your skin,
The taste of your kiss,
The way you whisper in the dark.
Your hair all around me,
Baby, you surround me.
You touch every place in my heart.
Oh, it feels like the first time every time.
I wanna spend the whole night in your eyes.
(To Chorus:)

THE DANCE

Words and Music by Tony Arata
Arranged by Dan Coates

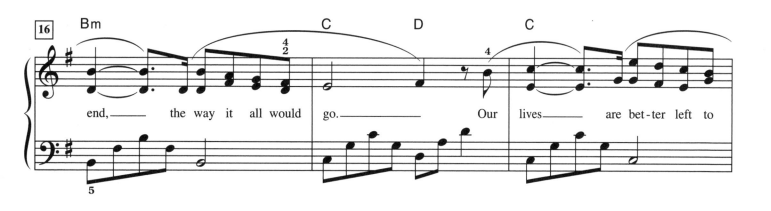

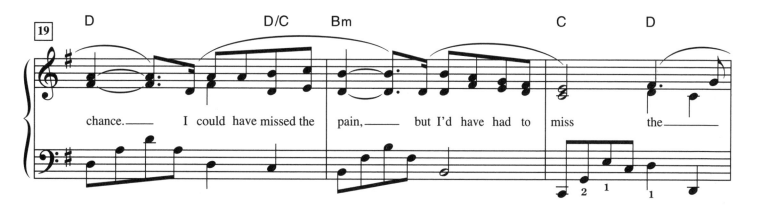

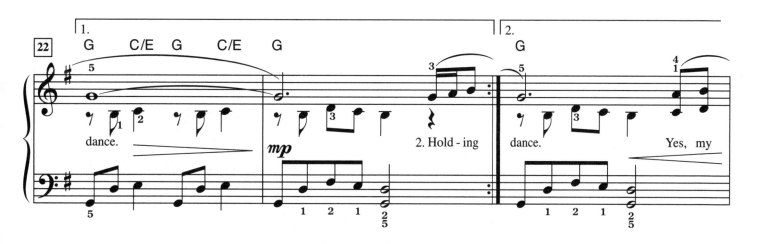

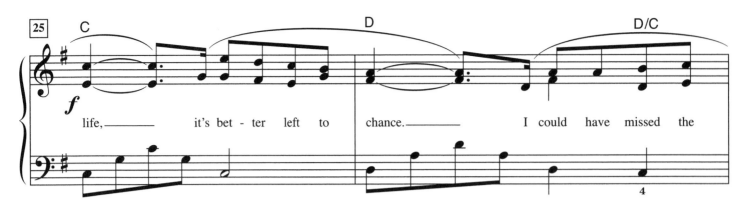

life,_____ it's bet-ter left to chance._____ I could have missed the

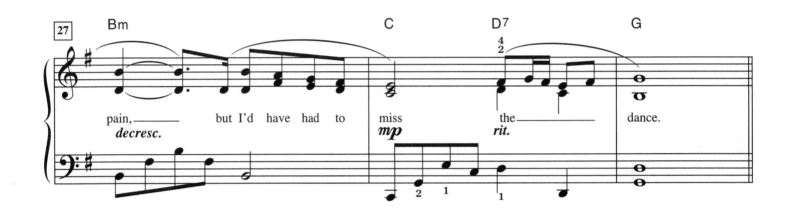

pain,_____ but I'd have had to miss the_____ dance.

decresc.

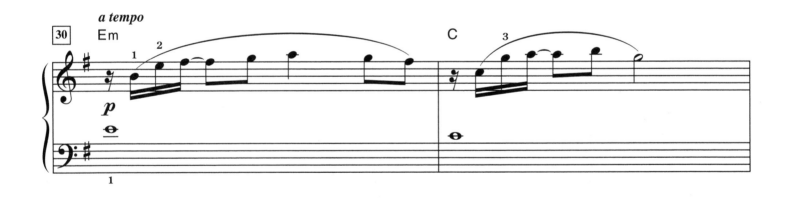

a tempo

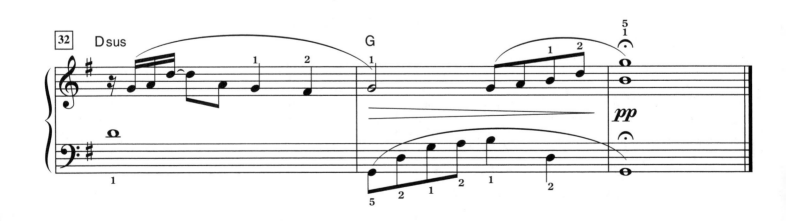

DON'T ROCK THE JUKEBOX

Words and Music by Alan Jackson,
Roger Murrah and Keith Stegall
Arranged by Dan Coates

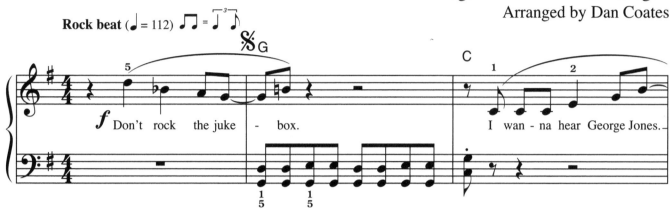

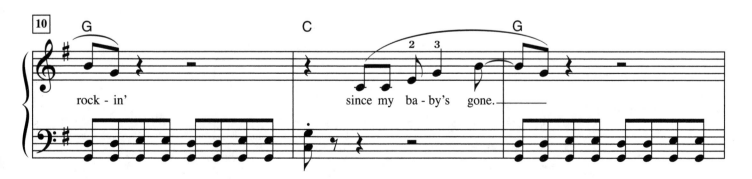

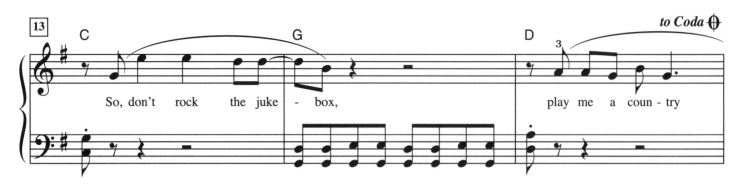

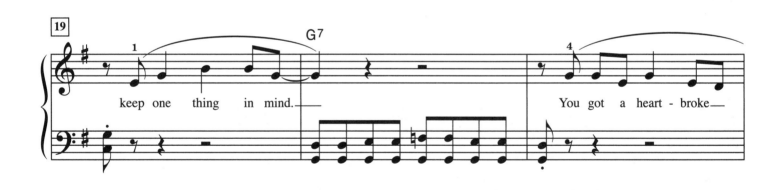

HOW DO I LIVE

Words and Music by Diane Warren
Arranged by Dan Coates

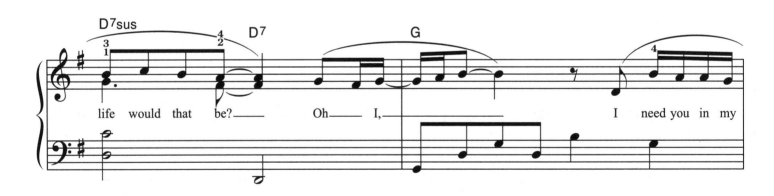

13

Verse 2:
Without you, there'd be no sun in my sky,
There would be no love in my life,
There'd be no world left for me.
And I, baby, I don't know what I would do,
I'd be lost if I lost you.
If you ever leave,
Baby, you would take away everything
Real in my life.
And tell me now...
(To Chorus):

I SWEAR

Words and Music by
Gary Baker and Frank Myers
Arranged by Dan Coates

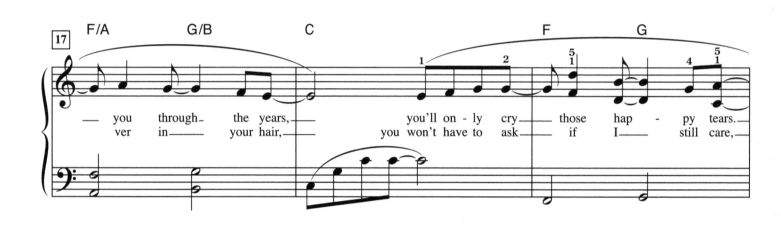

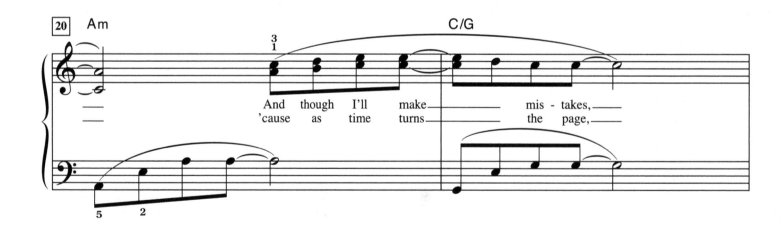

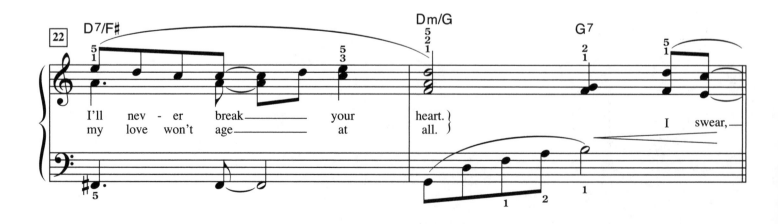

Chorus:

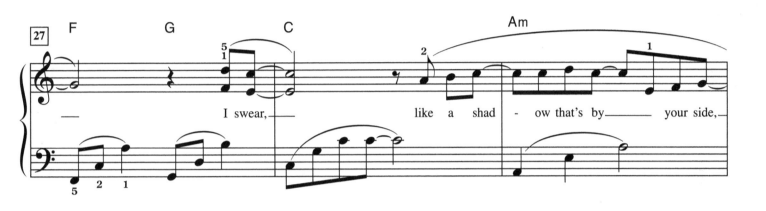

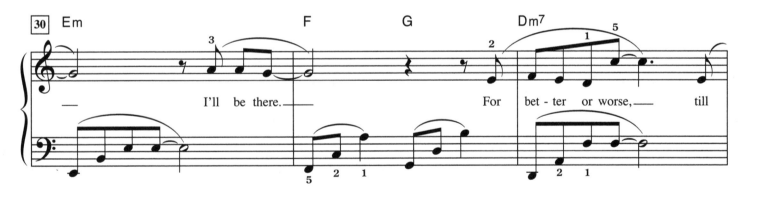

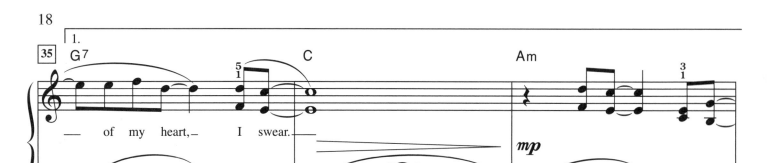

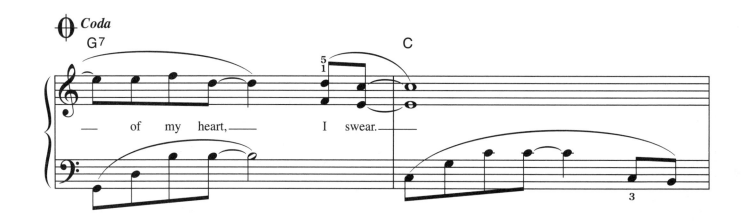

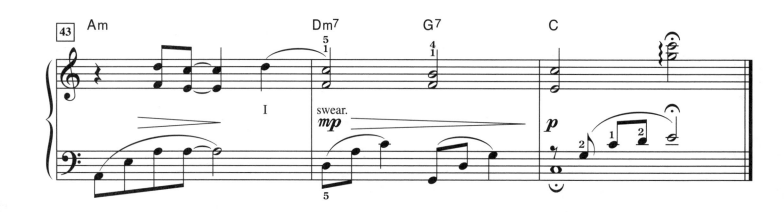

I'M TAKING THE WHEEL

Words and Music by
John Shanks and Kristyn Osborn
Arranged by Dan Coates

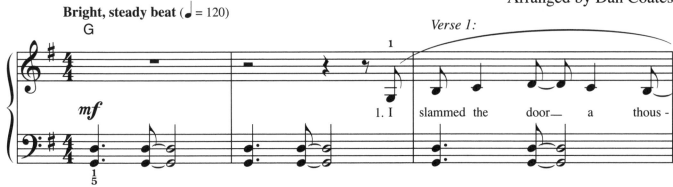

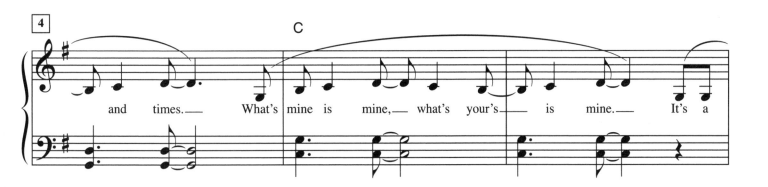

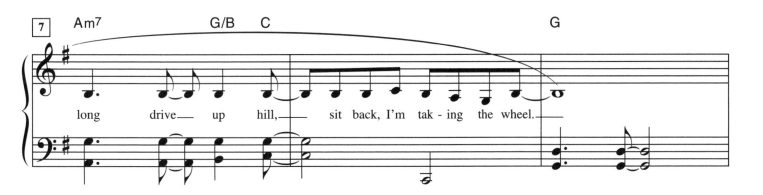

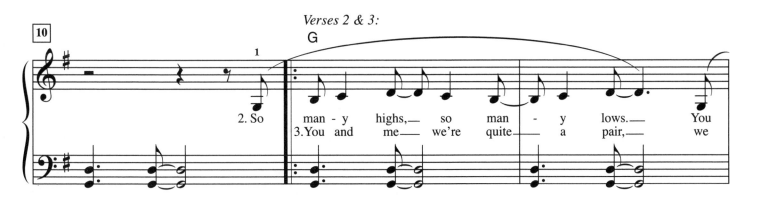

INSIDE YOUR HEAVEN

Words and Music by
Andreas Carlsson, Per Nylen and Savan Kotecha
Arranged by Dan Coates

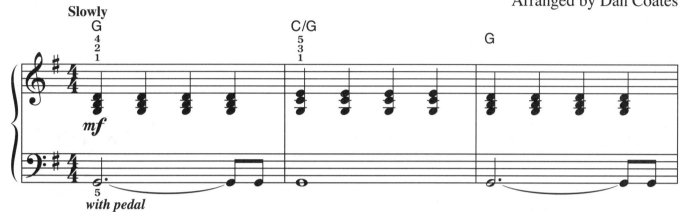

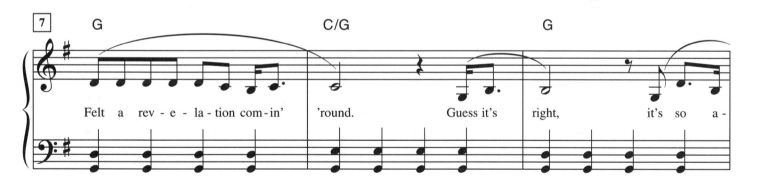

JUST TO HEAR YOU SAY THAT YOU LOVE ME

Words and Music by Dianne Warren
Arranged by Dan Coates

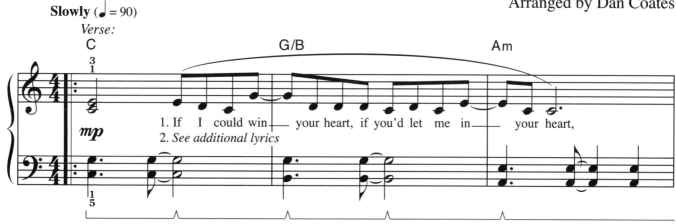

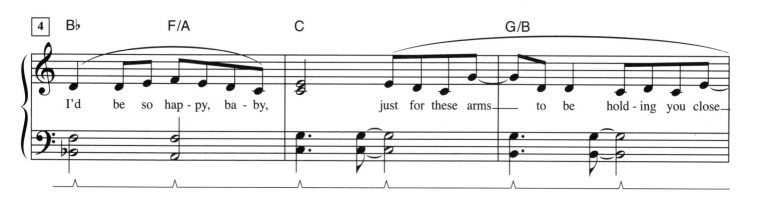

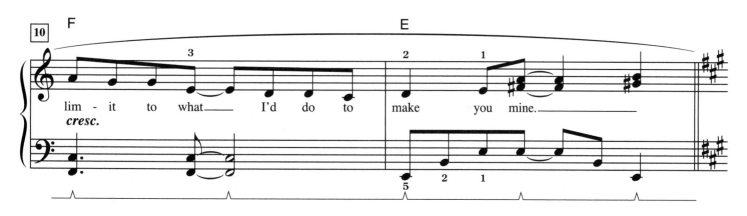

Verse 2:
If I could taste your kiss,
There'd be no sweeter gift
Heaven could offer, baby.
I want to be the one
Living to give you love.
I'd walk across this world just to be
Close to you, 'cos
I want you close to me.
(To Chorus:)

LET ME LET GO

Words and Music by
Dennis Morgan and Steve Diamond
Arranged by Dan Coates

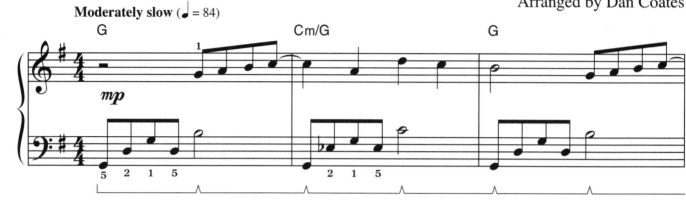

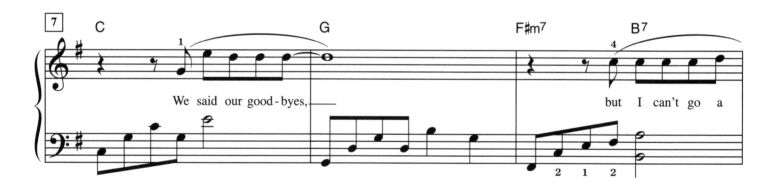

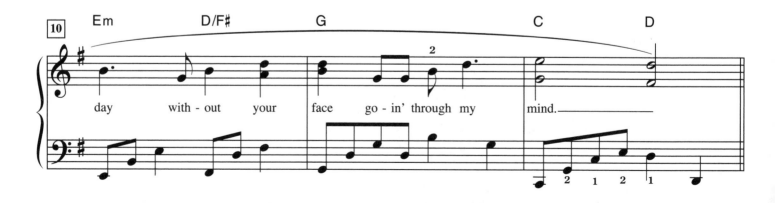

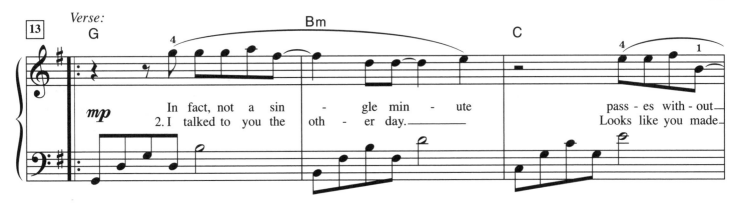

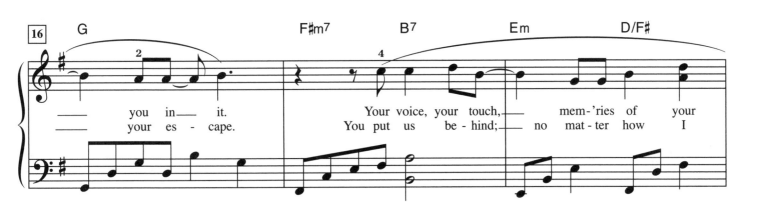

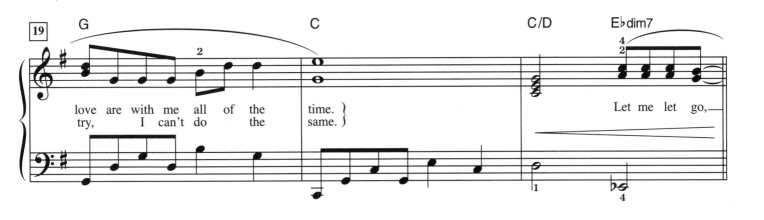

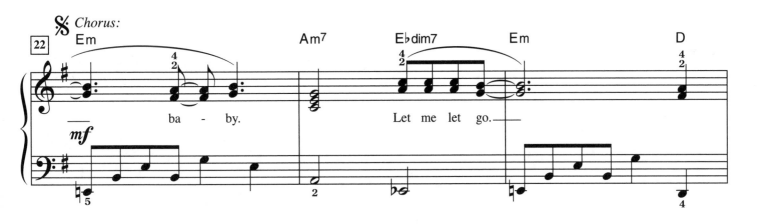

If this is for the best, why are you still in my heart, are you still in my

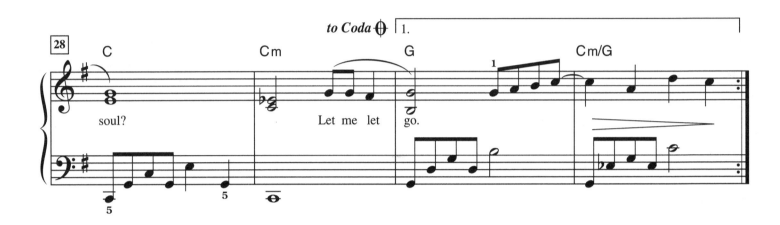

soul? Let me let go.

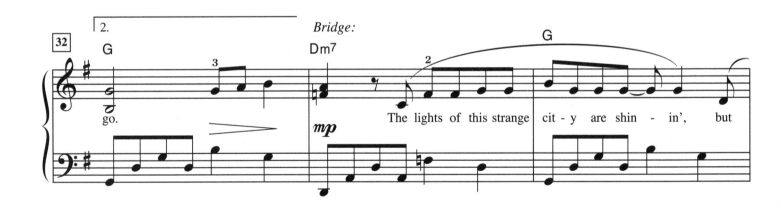

go. The lights of this strange cit - y are shin - in', but

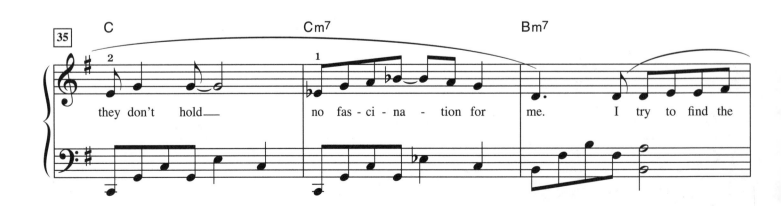

they don't hold___ no fas - ci - na - tion for me. I try to find the

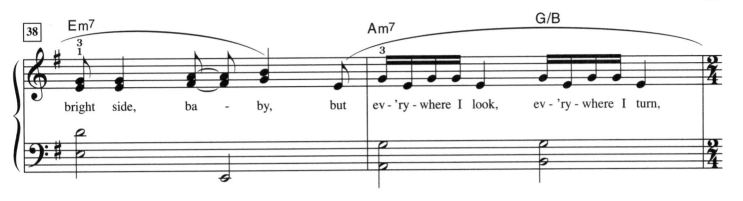

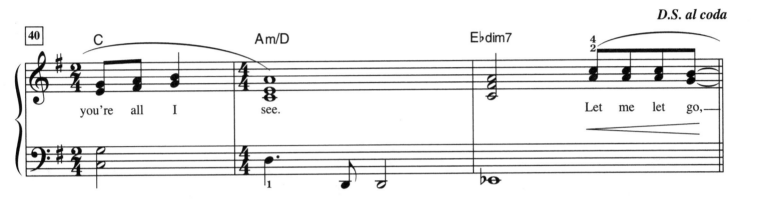

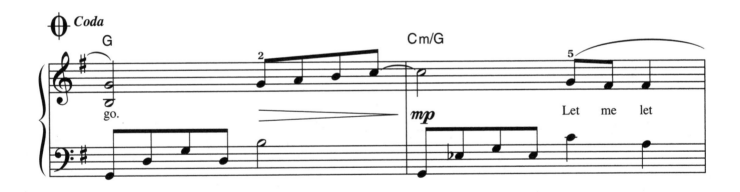

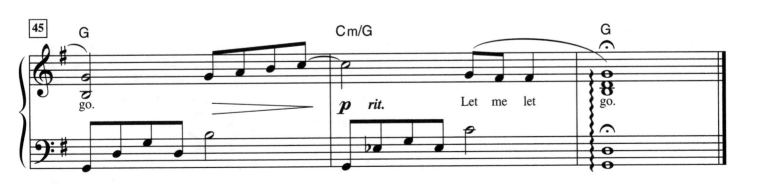

LIVE LIKE YOU WERE DYING

Words and Music by
Tim Nichols and Craig Wiseman
Arranged by Dan Coates

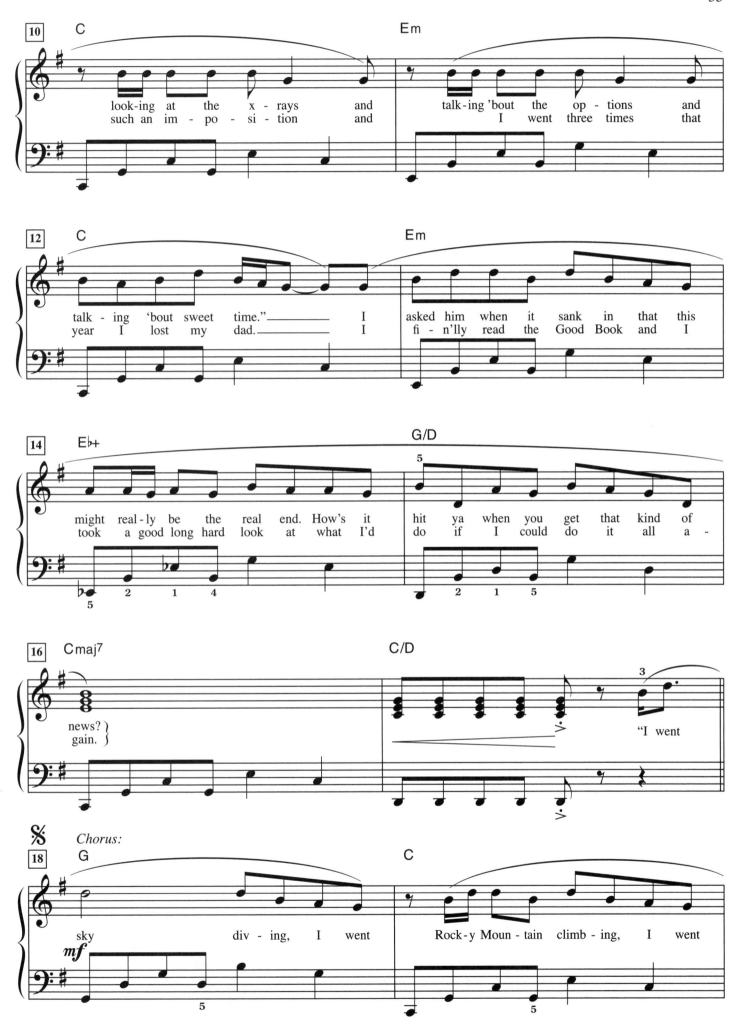

36

LOVE WILL ALWAYS WIN

Words and Music by
Wayne Kirkpatrick and Gordon Kennedy
Arranged by Dan Coates

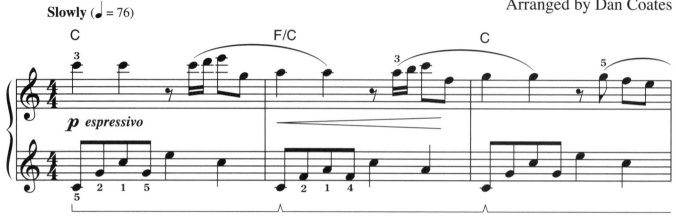

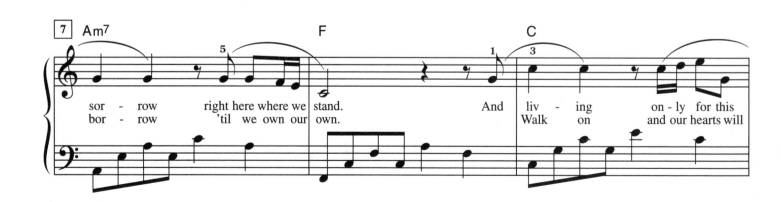

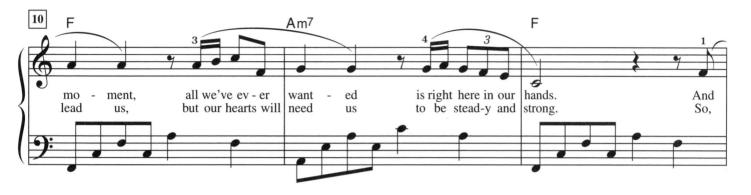

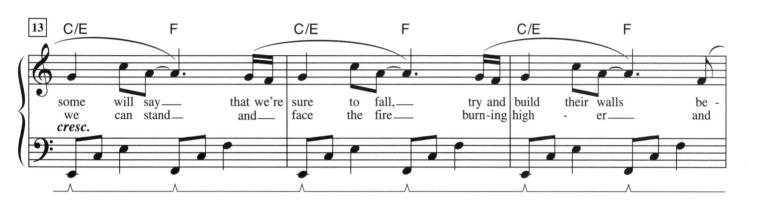

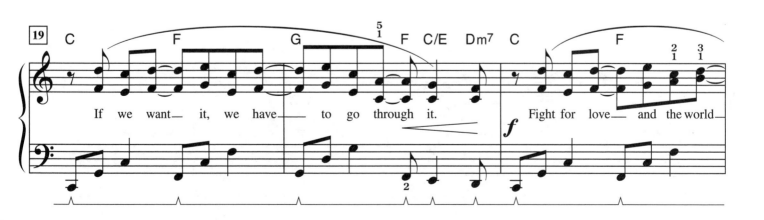

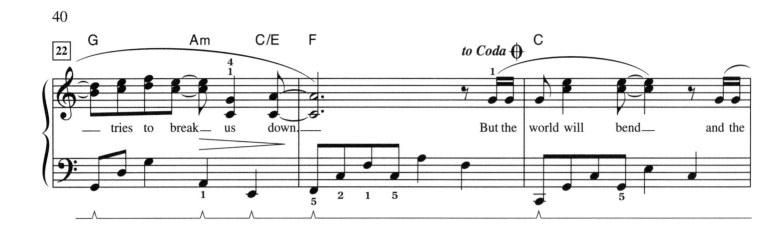

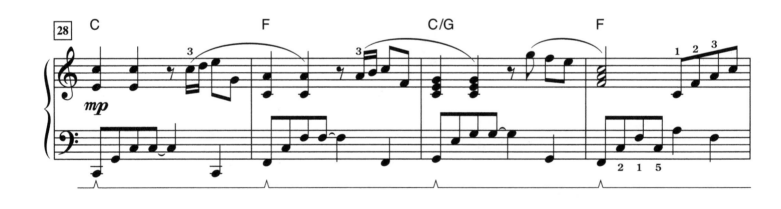

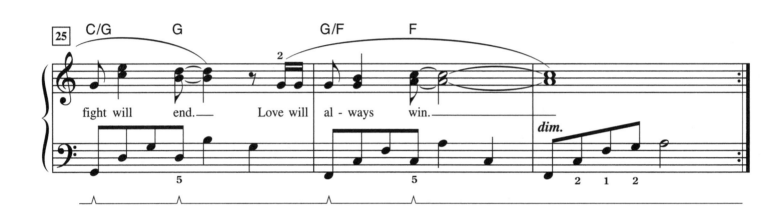

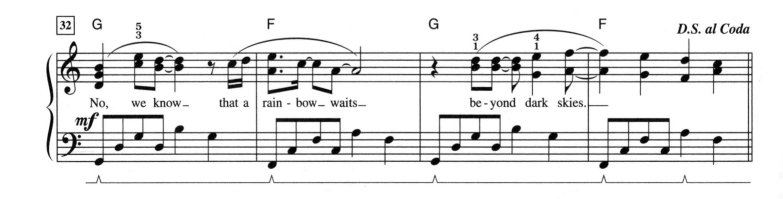

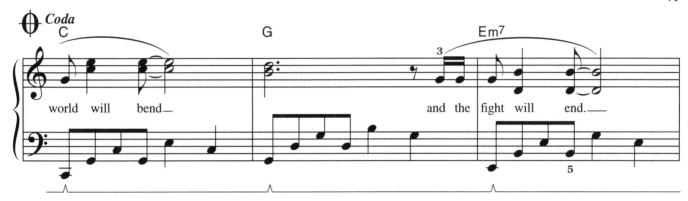

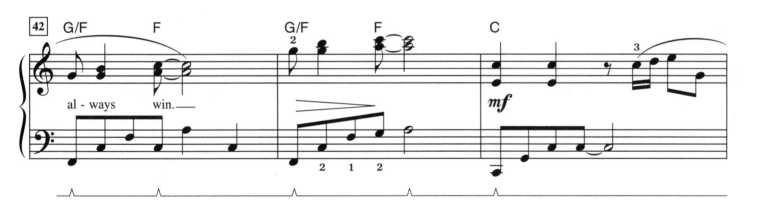

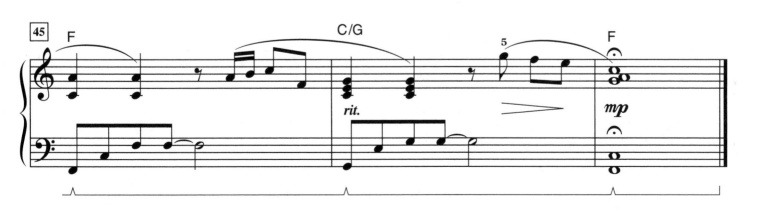

ONE MORE DAY

Words and Music by
Steven Dale Jones and Bobby Tomberlin
Arranged by Dan Coates

Moderately, with a steady beat ($\boldsymbol{\mathnormal{d}}$ = 69)

Verse:

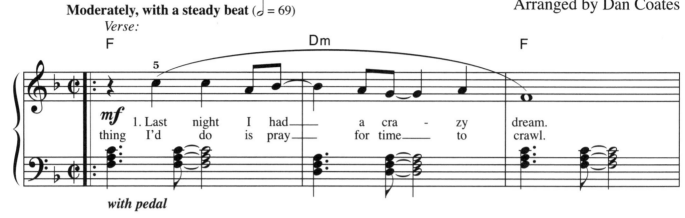

with pedal

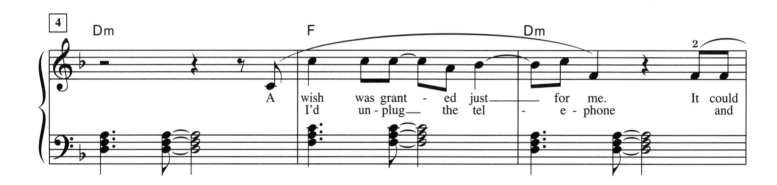

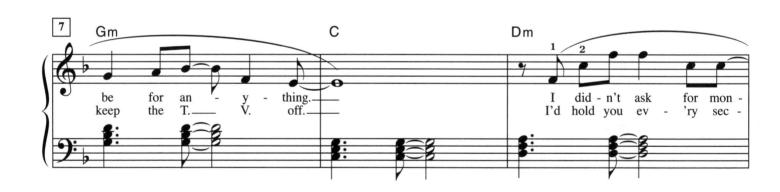

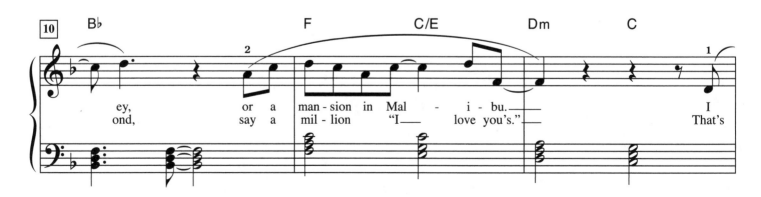

SOME HEARTS

Words and Music by Dianne Warren
Arranged by Dan Coates

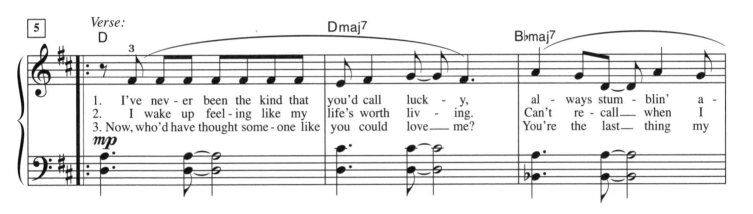

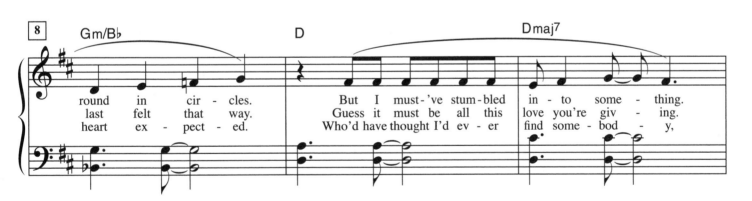

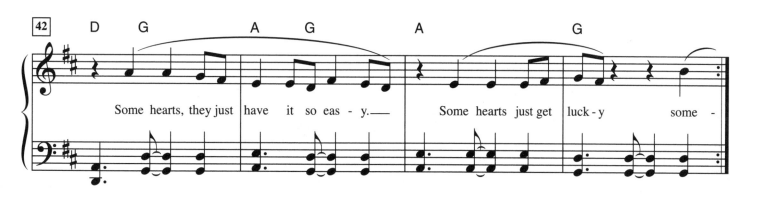

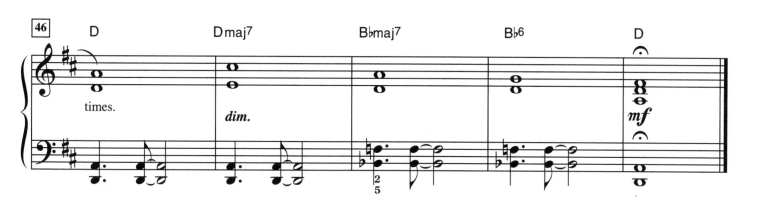

SOMEBODY LIKE YOU

Words and Music by
John Shanks and Keith Urban
Arranged by Dan Coates

Verse 2:

I'm letting go of all my lonely yesterdays
And forgiving myself for the mistakes I've made.
Now there's just one thing, the only thing I wanna do.
I wanna love somebody, love somebody like you.
(To Bridge:)

Verse 3:

I used to run in circles, goin' nowhere fast.
I'd take one step forward, end up two steps back.
I couldn't walk a straight line even if I wanted to,
But I wanna love somebody, love somebody like you.

Verse 4:
Instrumental solo
(To Bridge:)

Verse 5:

Sometimes it's hard for me to understand,
But you're teachin' me to be a better man.
Don't want to take this life for granted like I used to do.
I wanna love somebody, love somebody like you.

SUNSHINE ON MY SHOULDERS

Words by John Denver
Music by John Denver, Mike Taylor and Dick Kniss
Arranged by Dan Coates

THIS KISS

Words and Music by
Robin Lerner, Annie Roboff
and Beth Nielsen Chapman
Arranged by Dan Coates

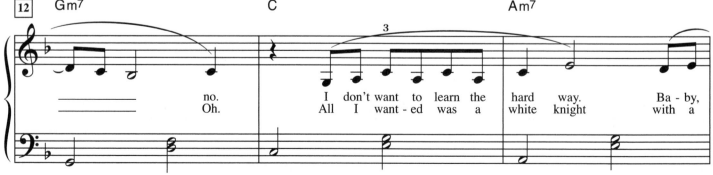

WHEN I THINK ABOUT ANGELS

Words and Music by Roxie Dean,
Sonny Tillis and Jamie O'Neal
Arranged by Dan Coates

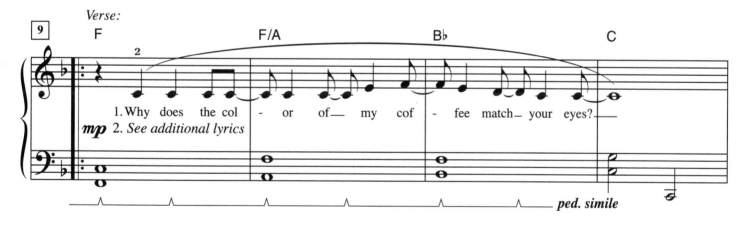

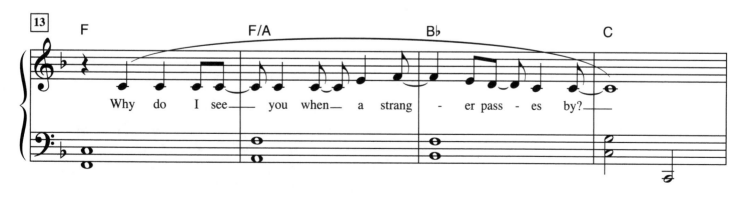

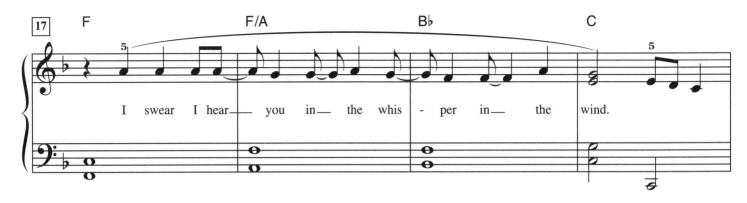

I swear I hear you in the whis - per in the wind.

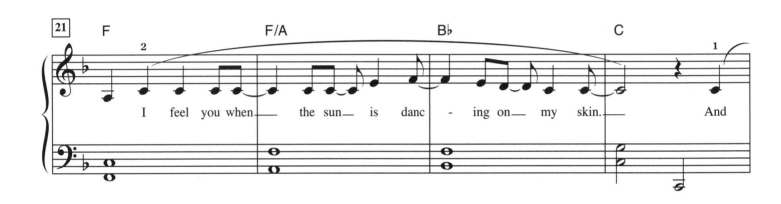

I feel you when the sun is danc - ing on my skin. And

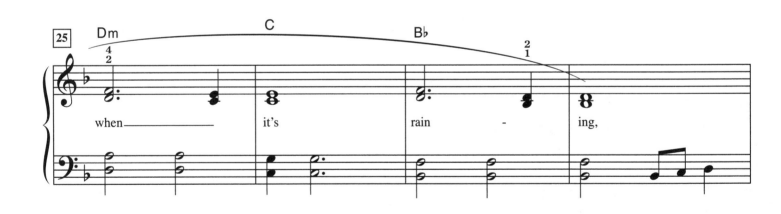

when it's rain - ing,

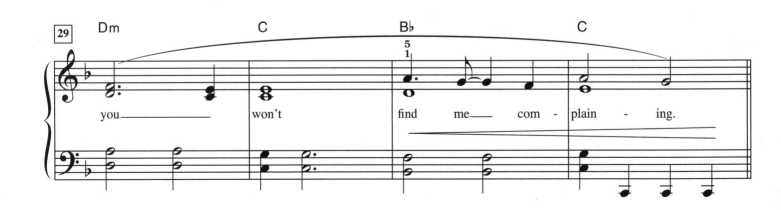

you won't find me com - plain - ing.

Chorus:

When I think a - bout rain,——— I think a - bout sing - ing.———

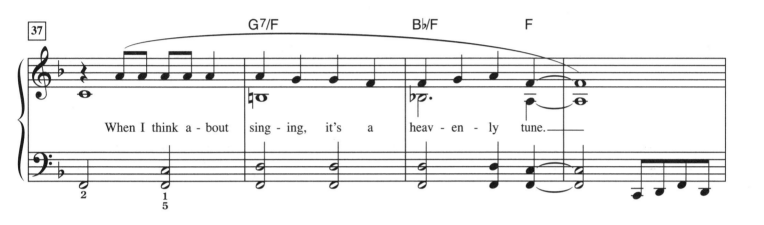

When I think a - bout sing - ing, it's a heav - en - ly tune.———

When I think a - bout heav - en, then I think a - bout an - gels.———

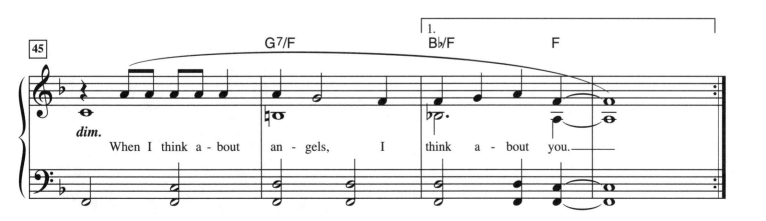

When I think a - bout an - gels, I think a - bout you.———

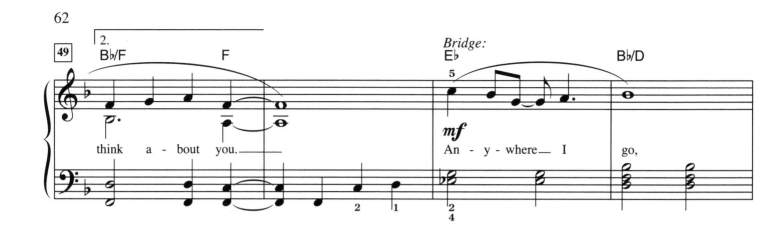

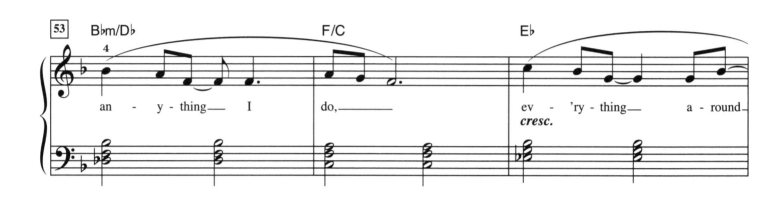

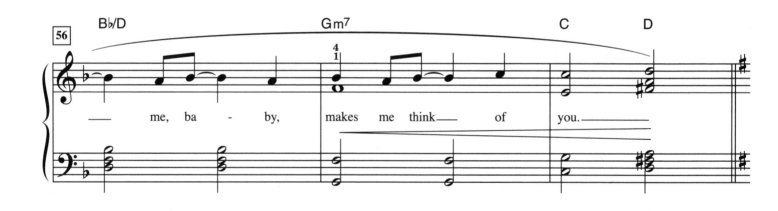

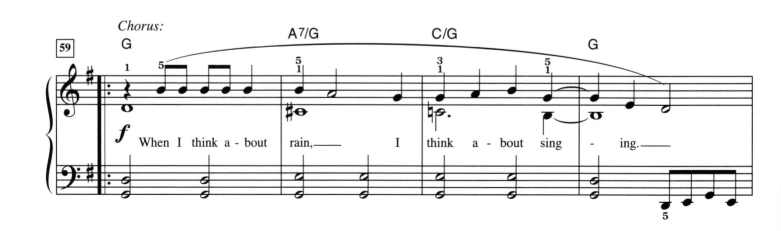

Verse 2:
The taste of sugar sure reminds me of your kiss.
I like the way they both linger on my lips.
Kisses remind me of a field of butterflies.
Must be the way the heart is fluttering inside.
Beautiful distraction,
You make every thought a chain reaction.
(To Chorus:)